Map Legend

Borders

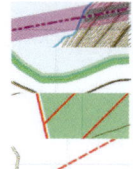
- Country border
- Natural Park border
- Military/restricted area
- Fence
- Gate

Roads & Paths

- Surfaced roads
- Dirt roads & tracks
- Walking trails
- Restricted/guided trails
- Obligatory walking direction
- Major hiking/trekking routes
- Downhill skiing routes & lifts

Natural Terrain

- Lakes, ponds
- Rivers; streams
- Waterfalls
- Wetland
- Wood
- Scrub
- Heath
- Meadow; grass
- Sand; beach
- Glacier
- Crevasse
- Cliffs; rocks; arete
- Scree; shingle
- Viewpoint
- Cave entrance

Man-made Features

- Farmland
- Orchard
- Power line
- Railroad

(Utilities)

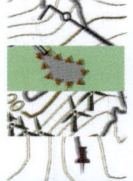
- Pipeline
- Quarry
- Wind turbine
- Radio mast, cell tower
- Lighthouse, buoy
- Cemetery
- Church

Amenities & Tourist Attractions

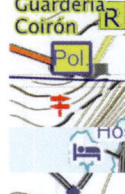
- Rangers post
- Police station; border control
- Tourist information
- Hotel, hostel
- Guest house; alpine hut; shelter
- Established campground; also staffed, commercial or otherwise regulated campsite
- Closed campsite
- Hospital
- Pharmacy
- Post office
- Playground
- Bank, ATM
- Monument, tourist attraction
- Museum

Transportation & Transport Amenities

- Car parking
- Fuel station
- Bus station/hub
- Bus stop
- Ferry & cruise ship routes
- Airport

Food & Water

- Cafe, restaurant, bakery
- Grocery store; supermarket
- Spring; drinking water fountain

All Elevations are in Meters
Mercator Projection

Sergio Mazitto Tourist Topo Maps

Available from
Amazon.com and other retailers

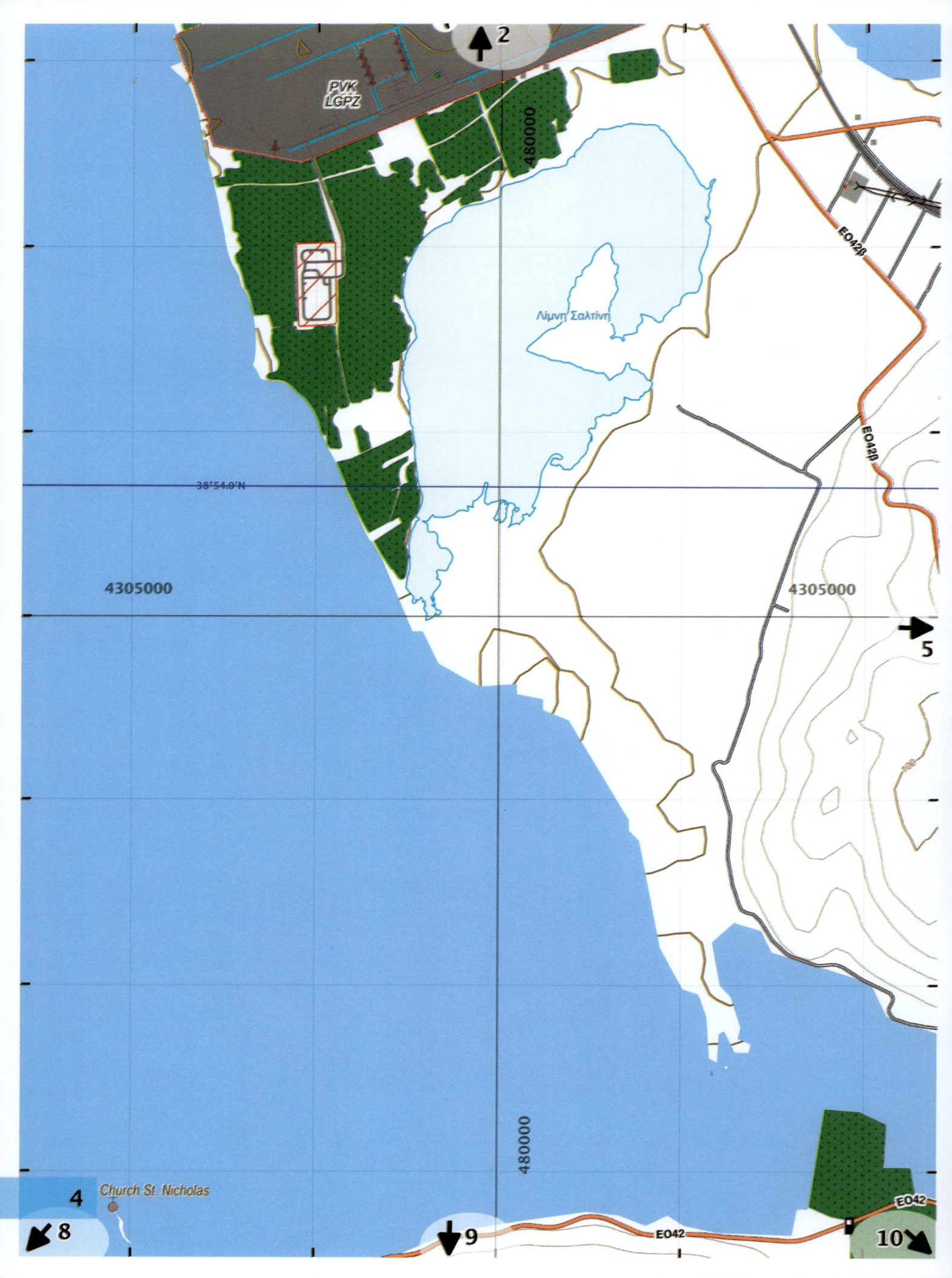

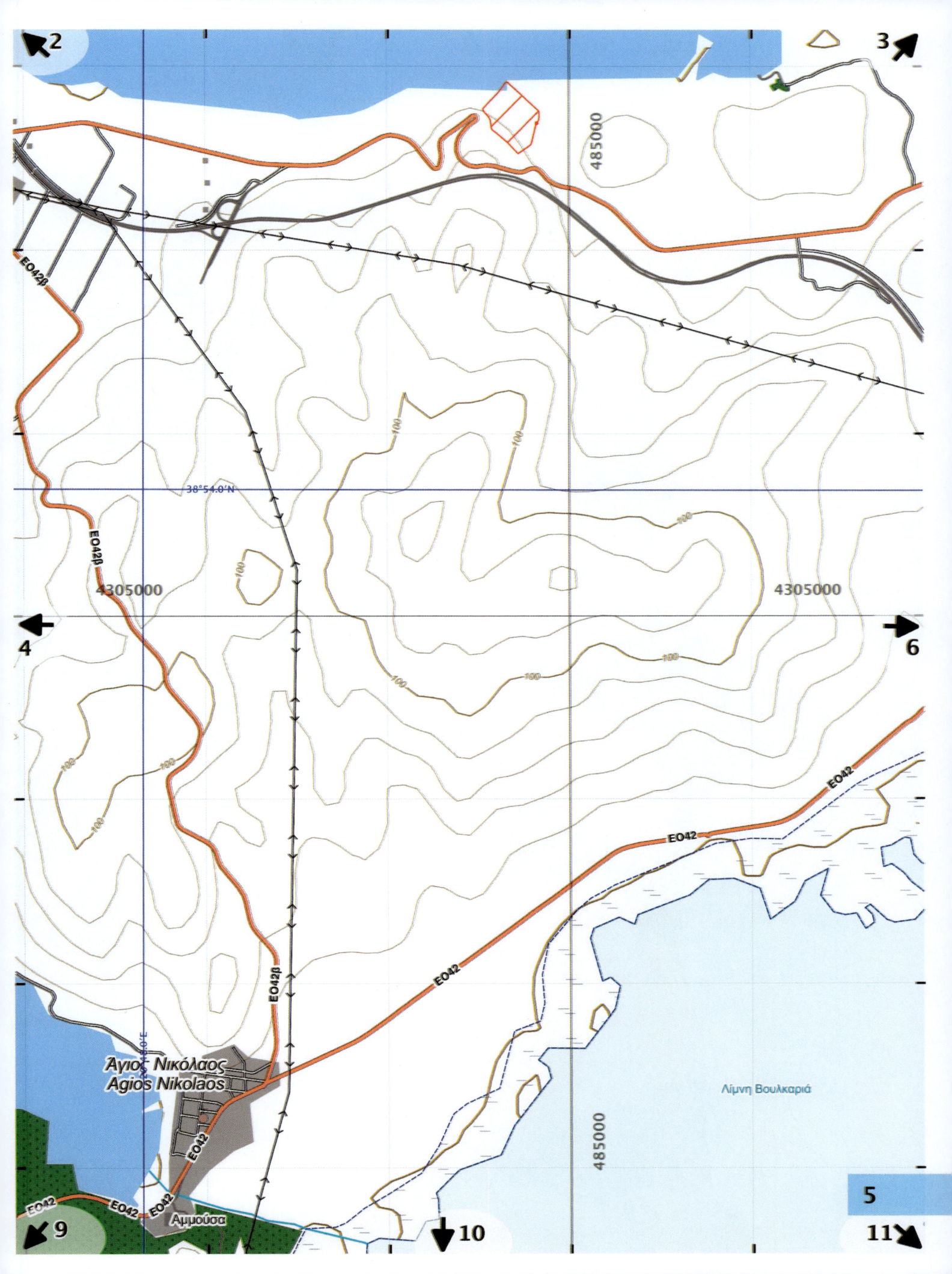

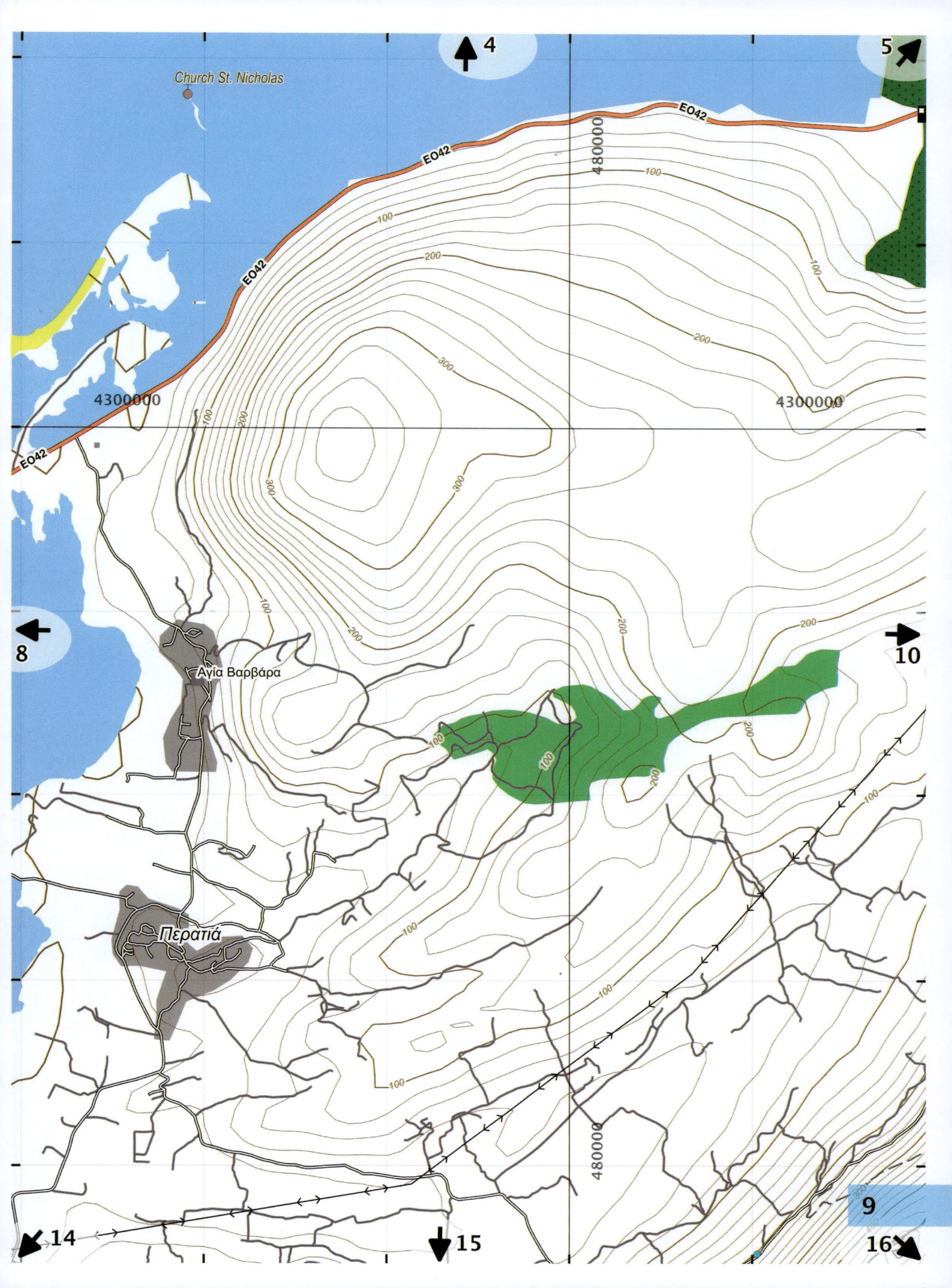

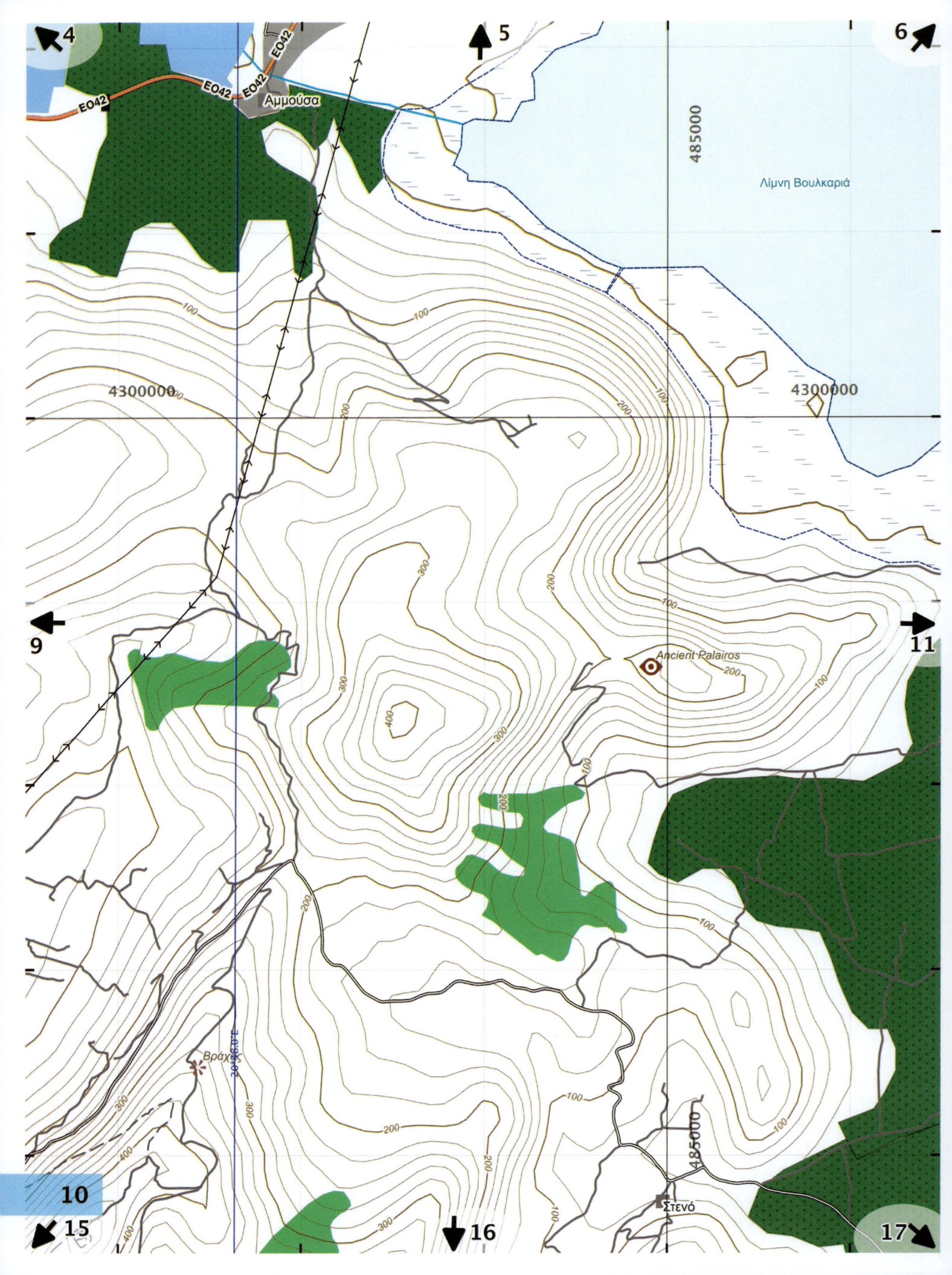

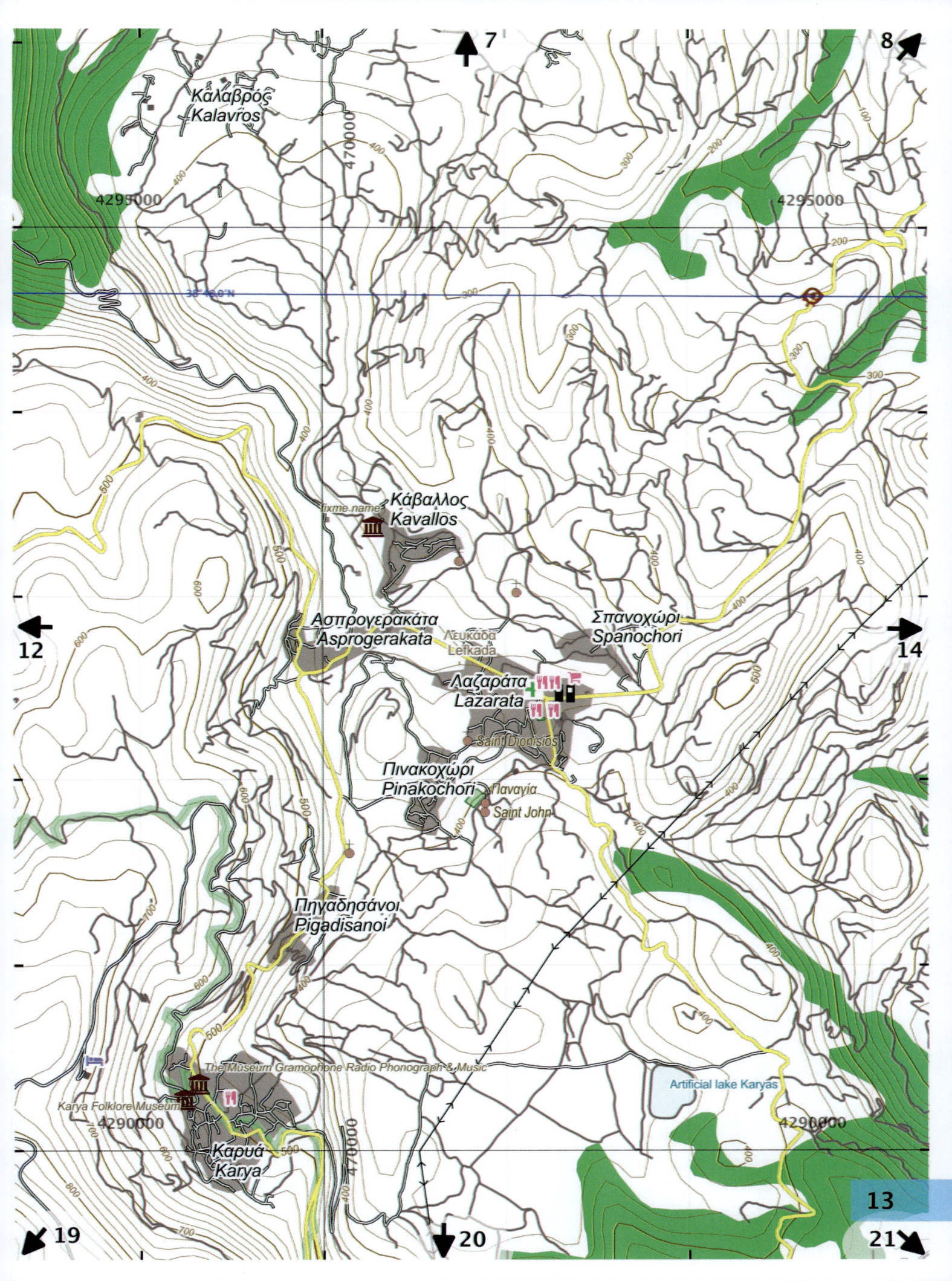

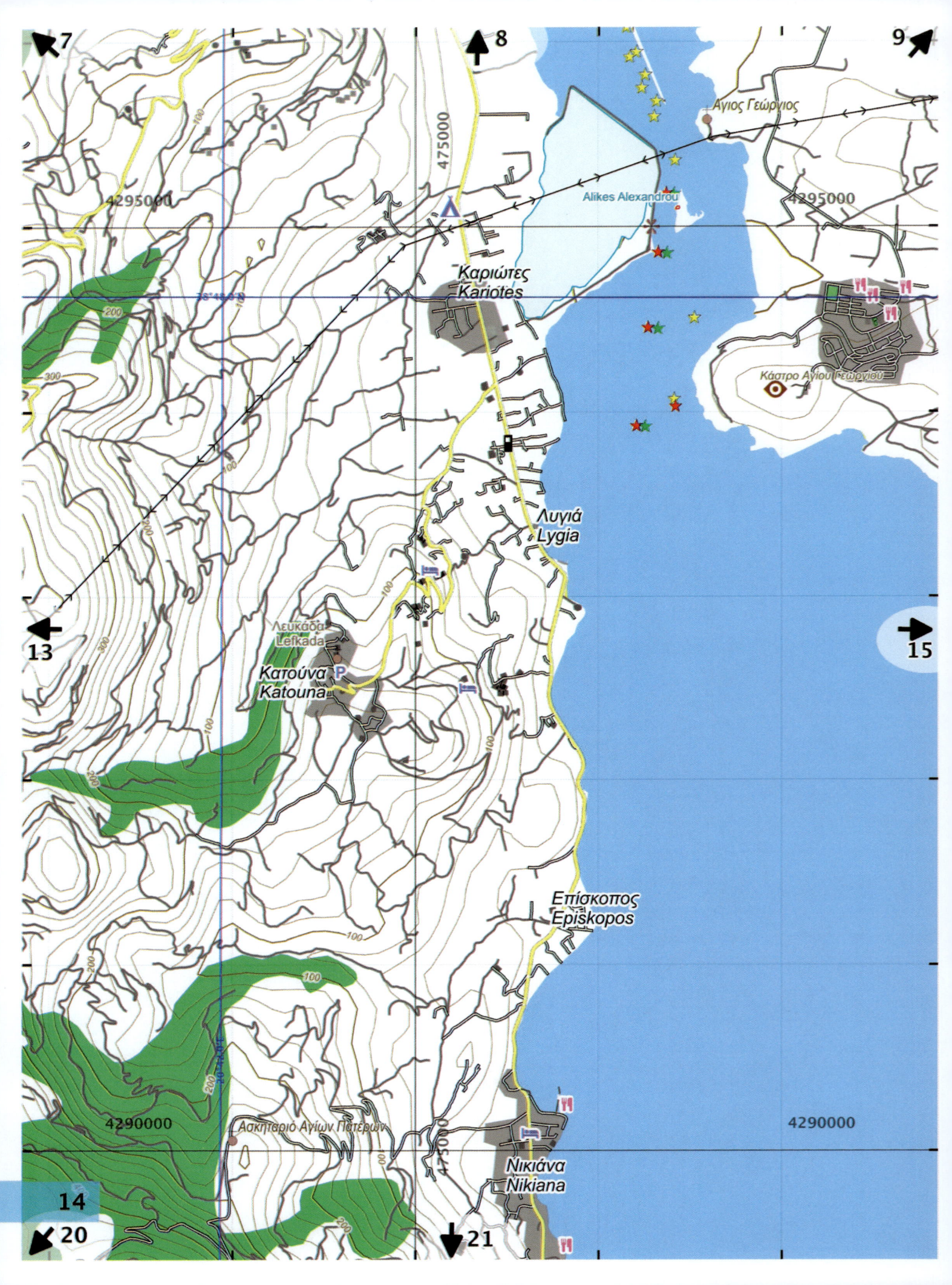

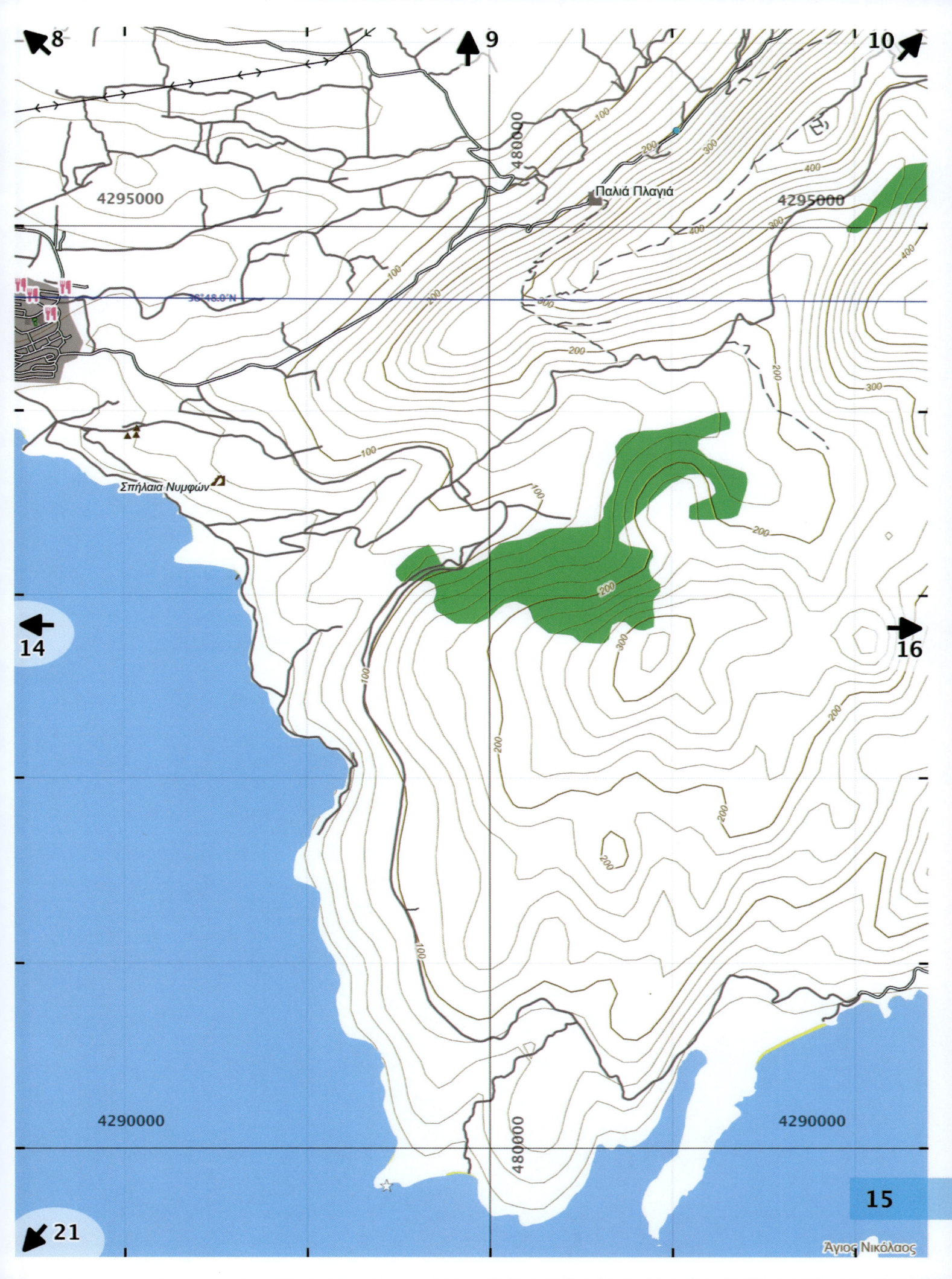

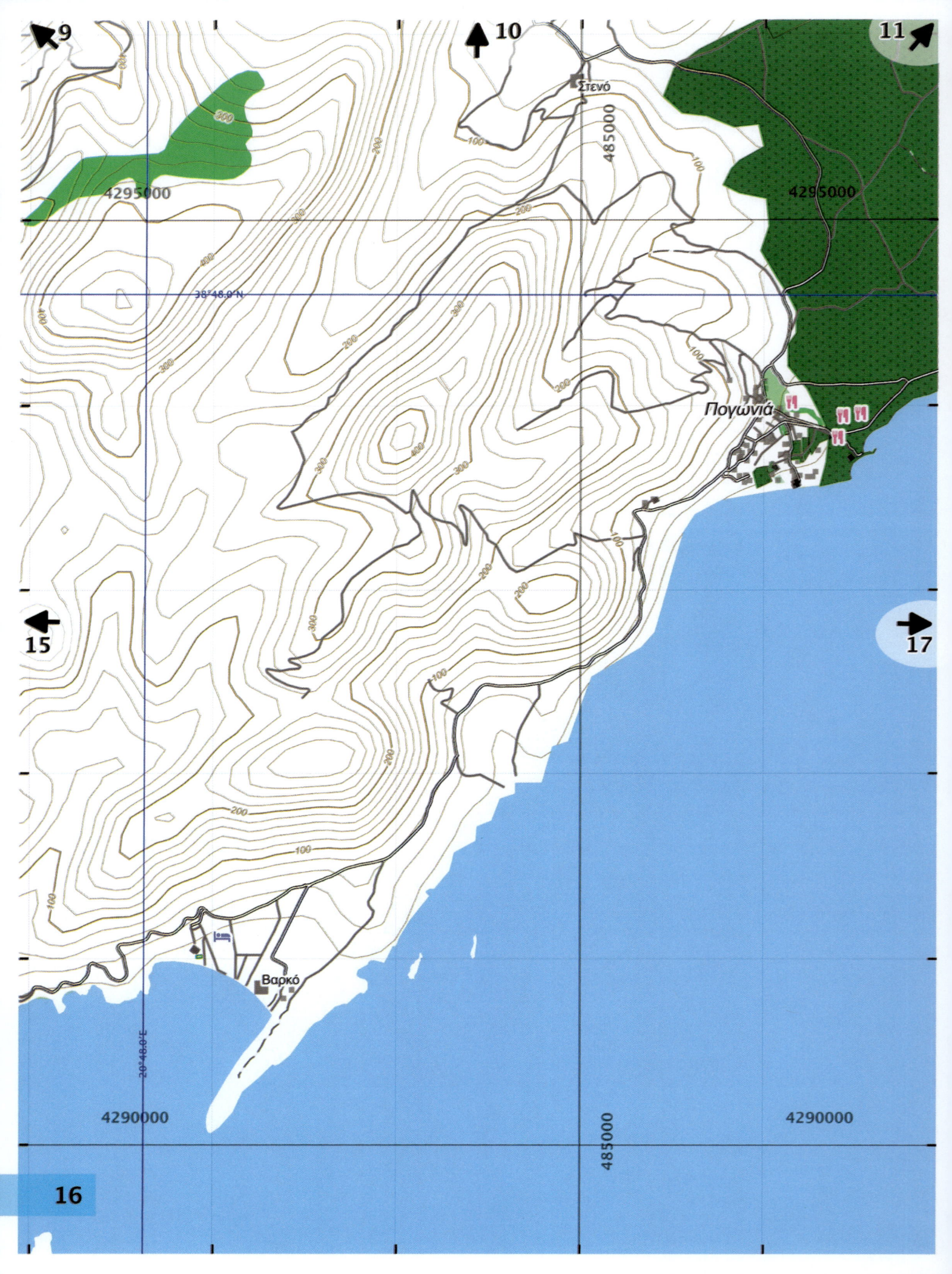

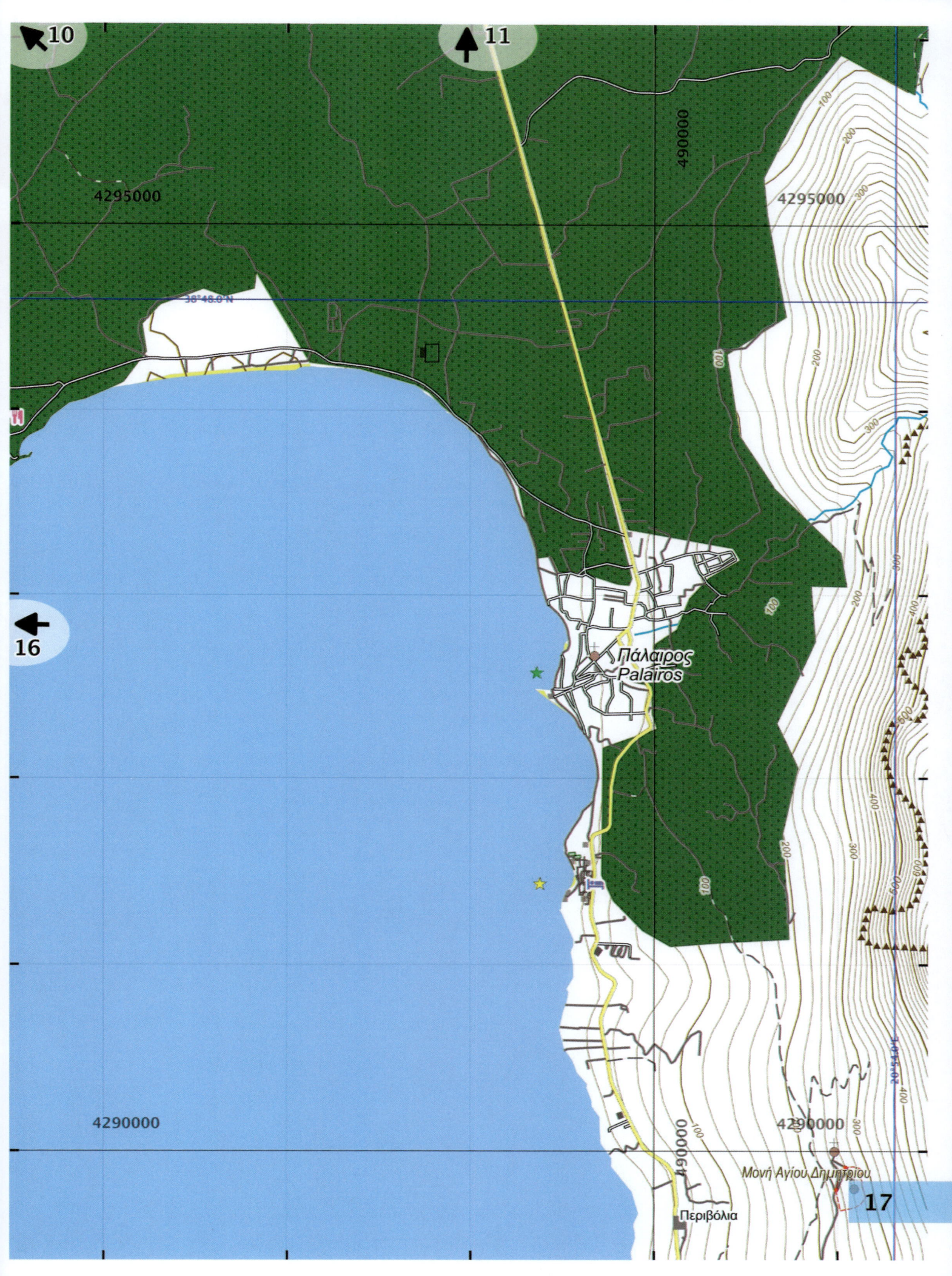

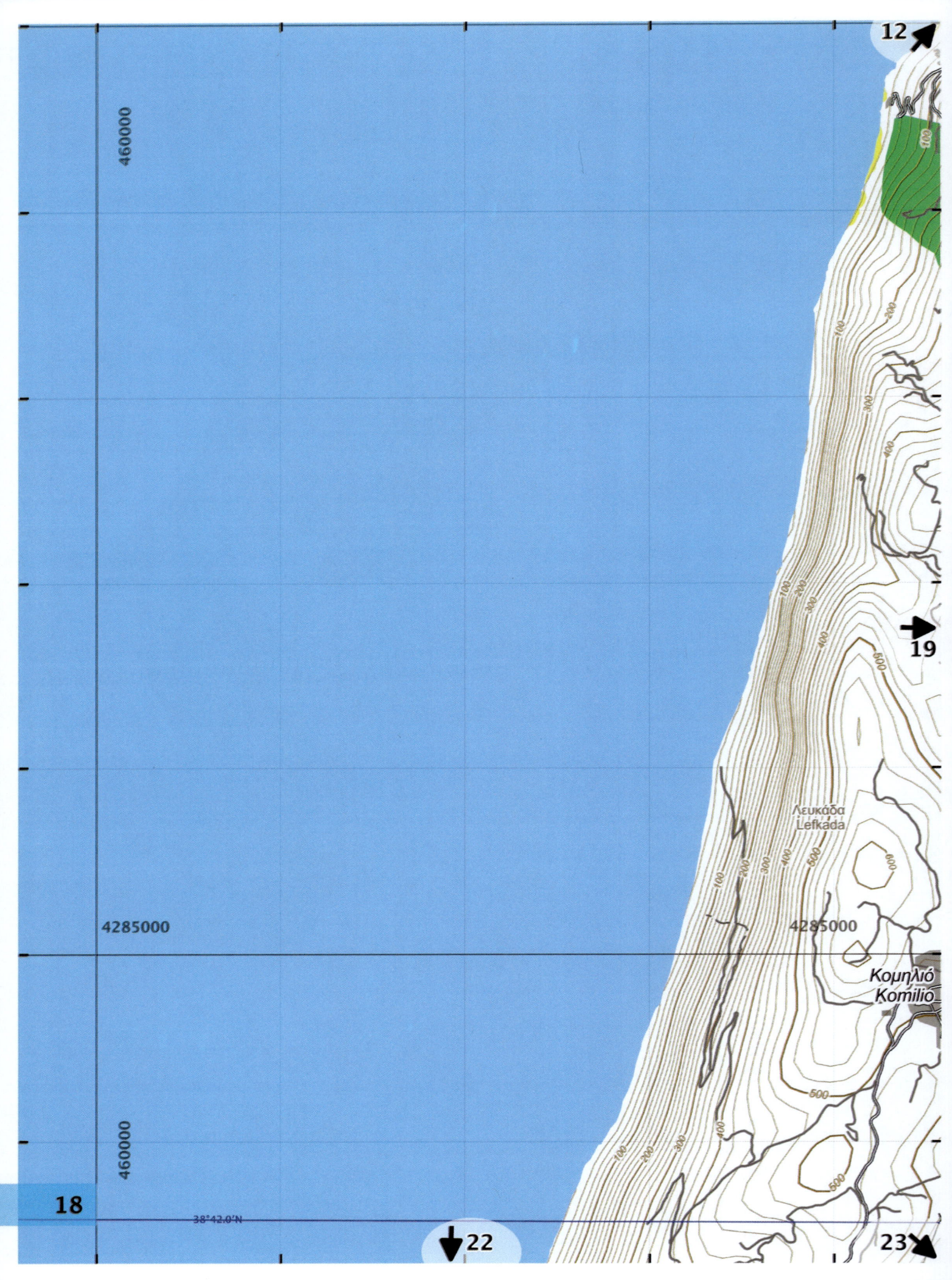

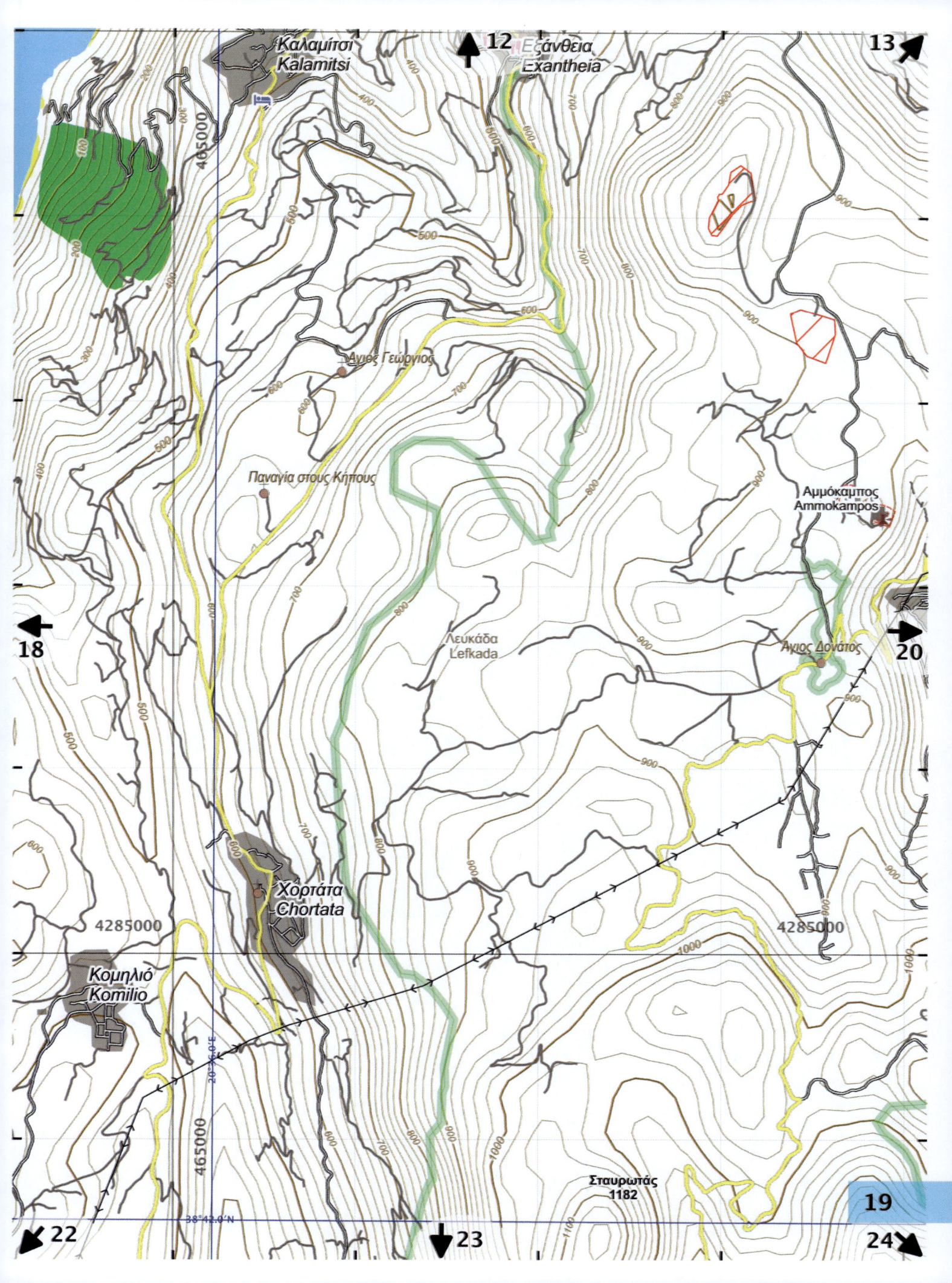

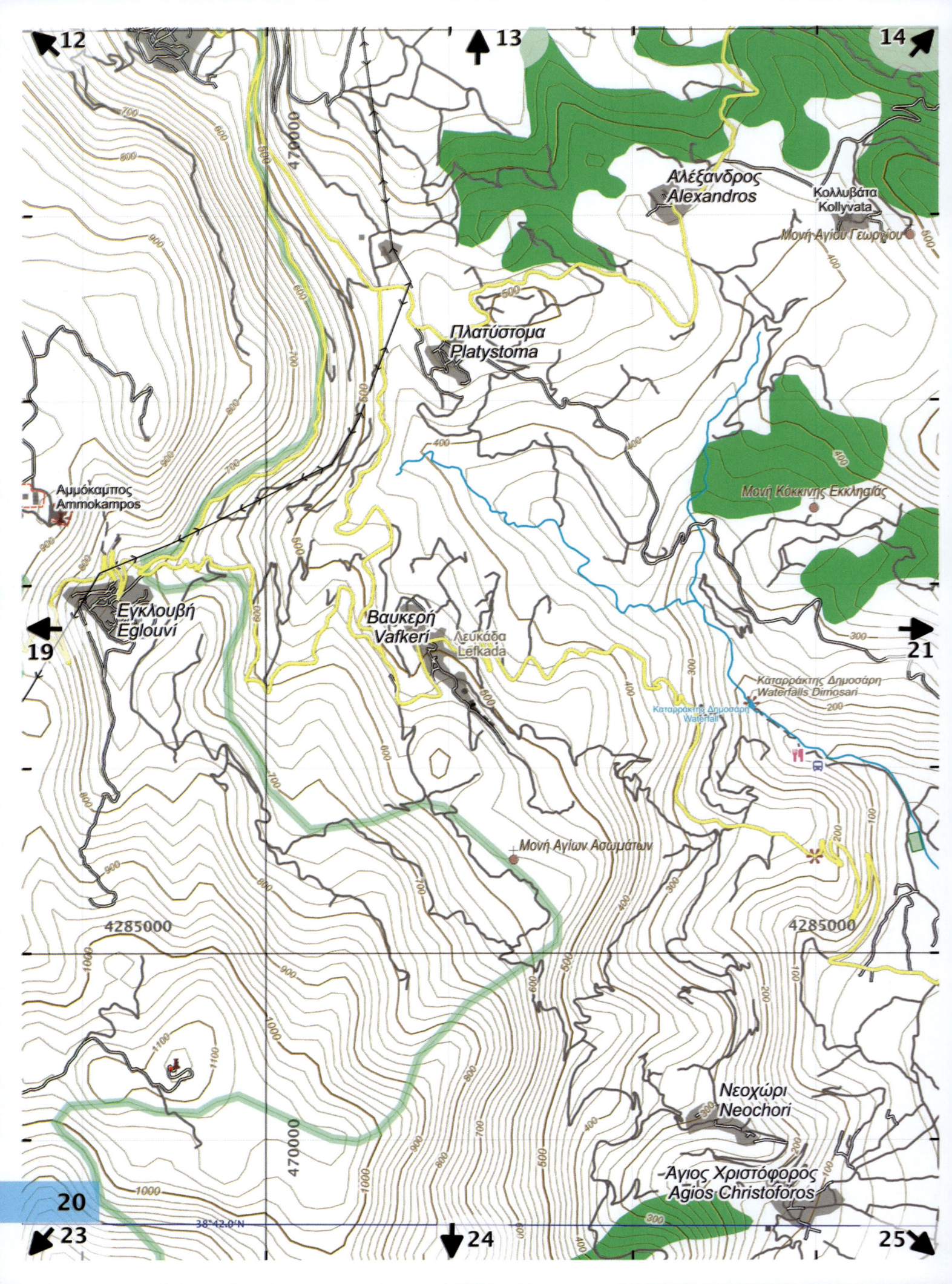

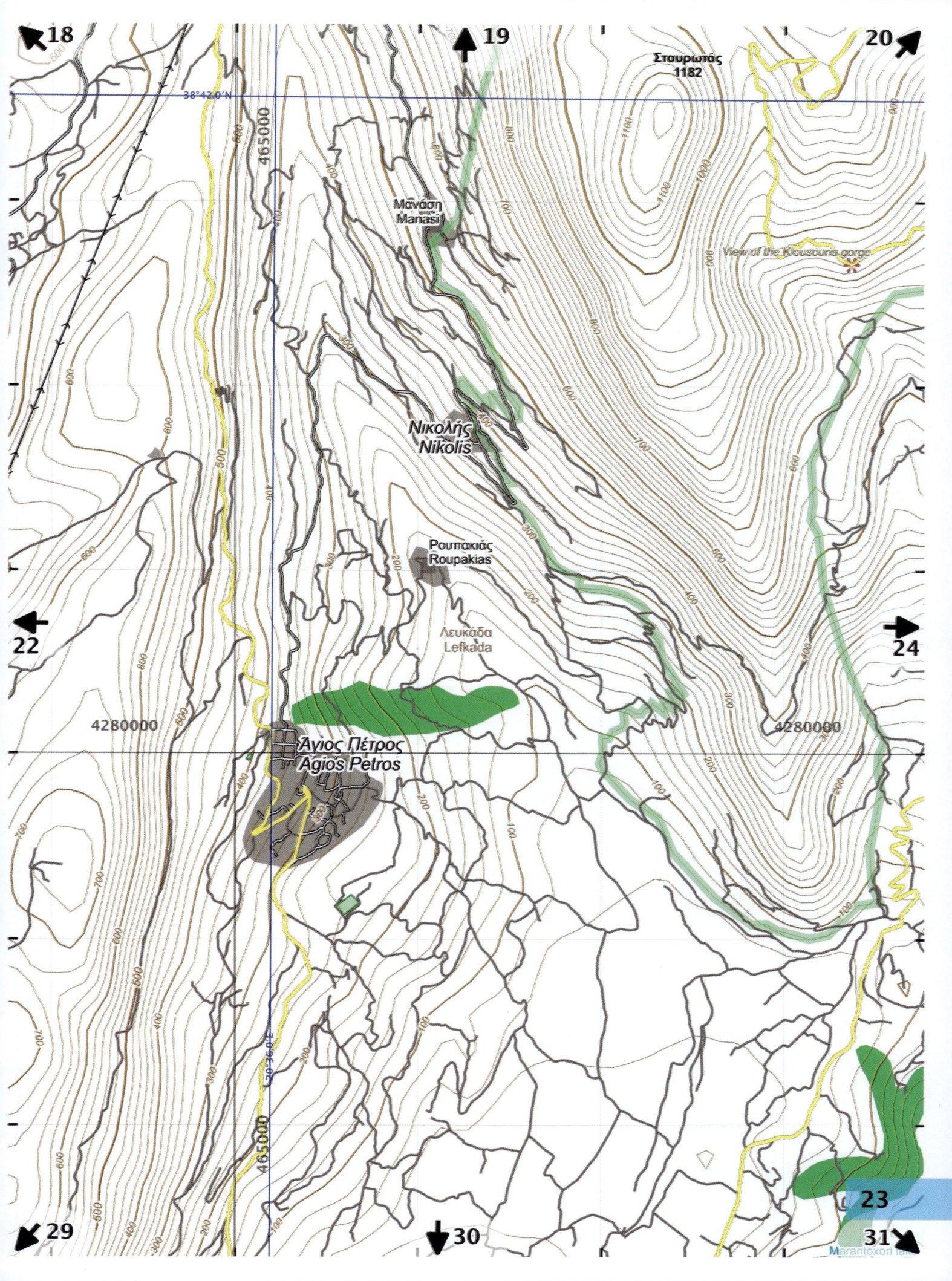

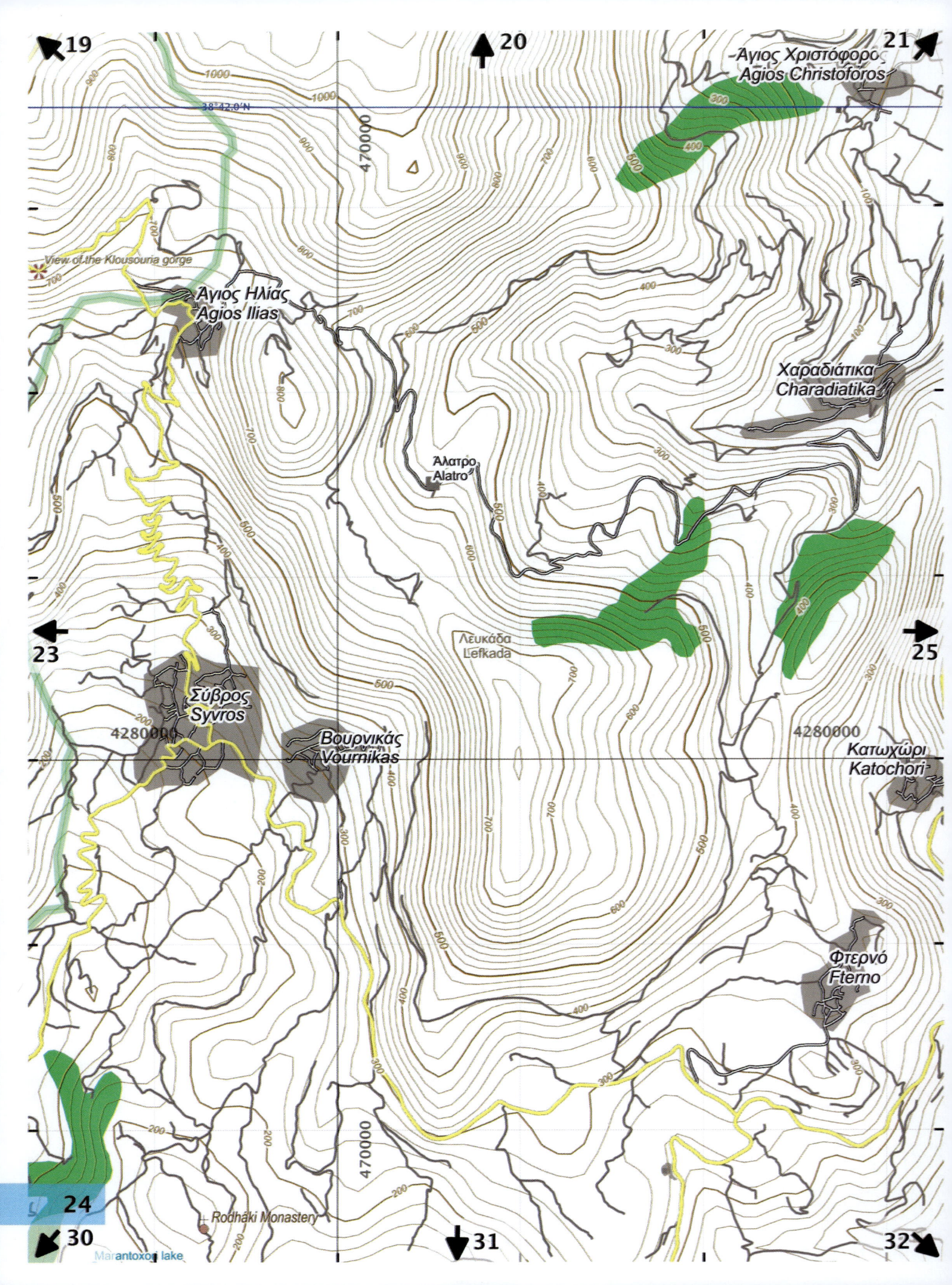

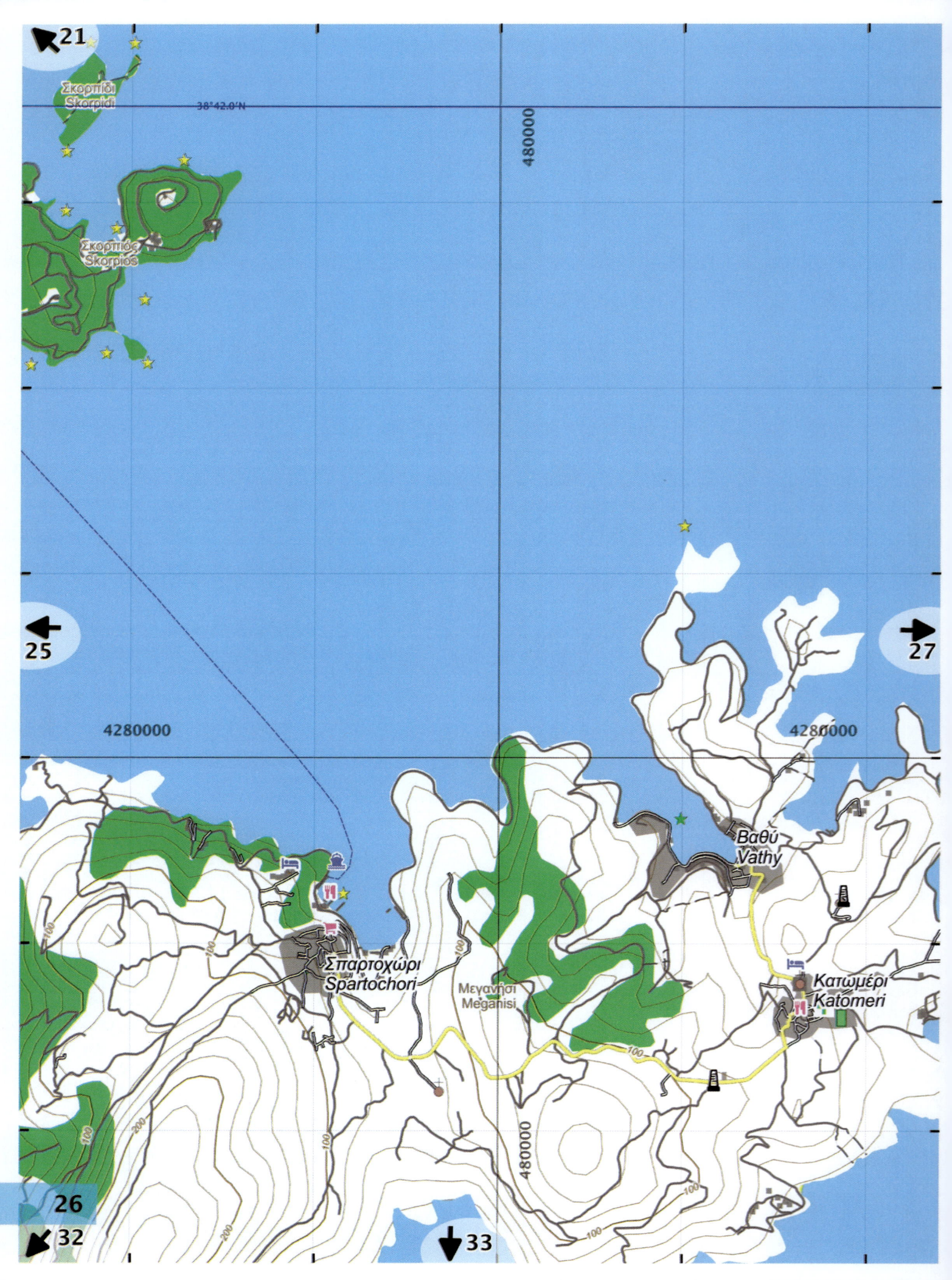

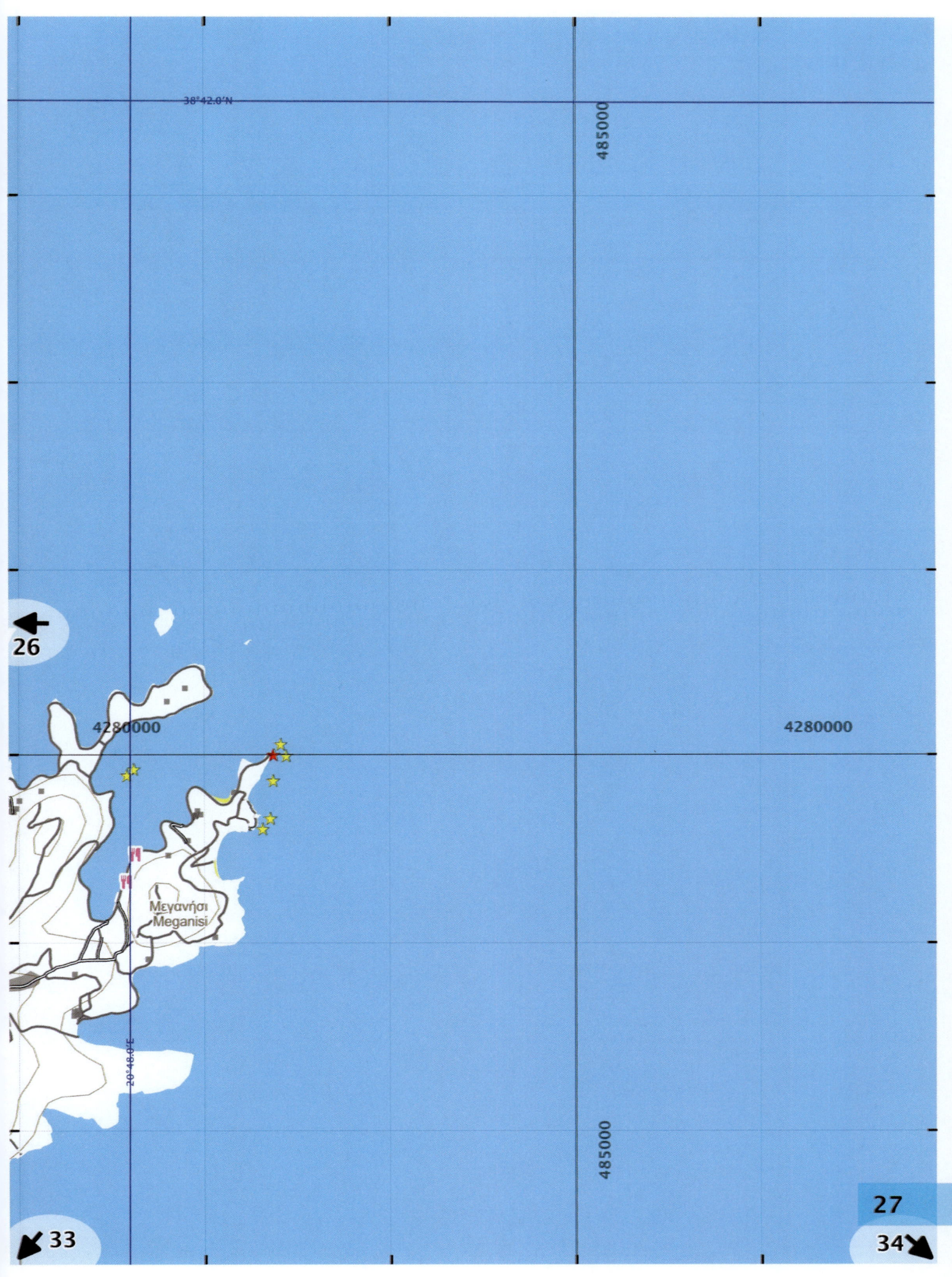

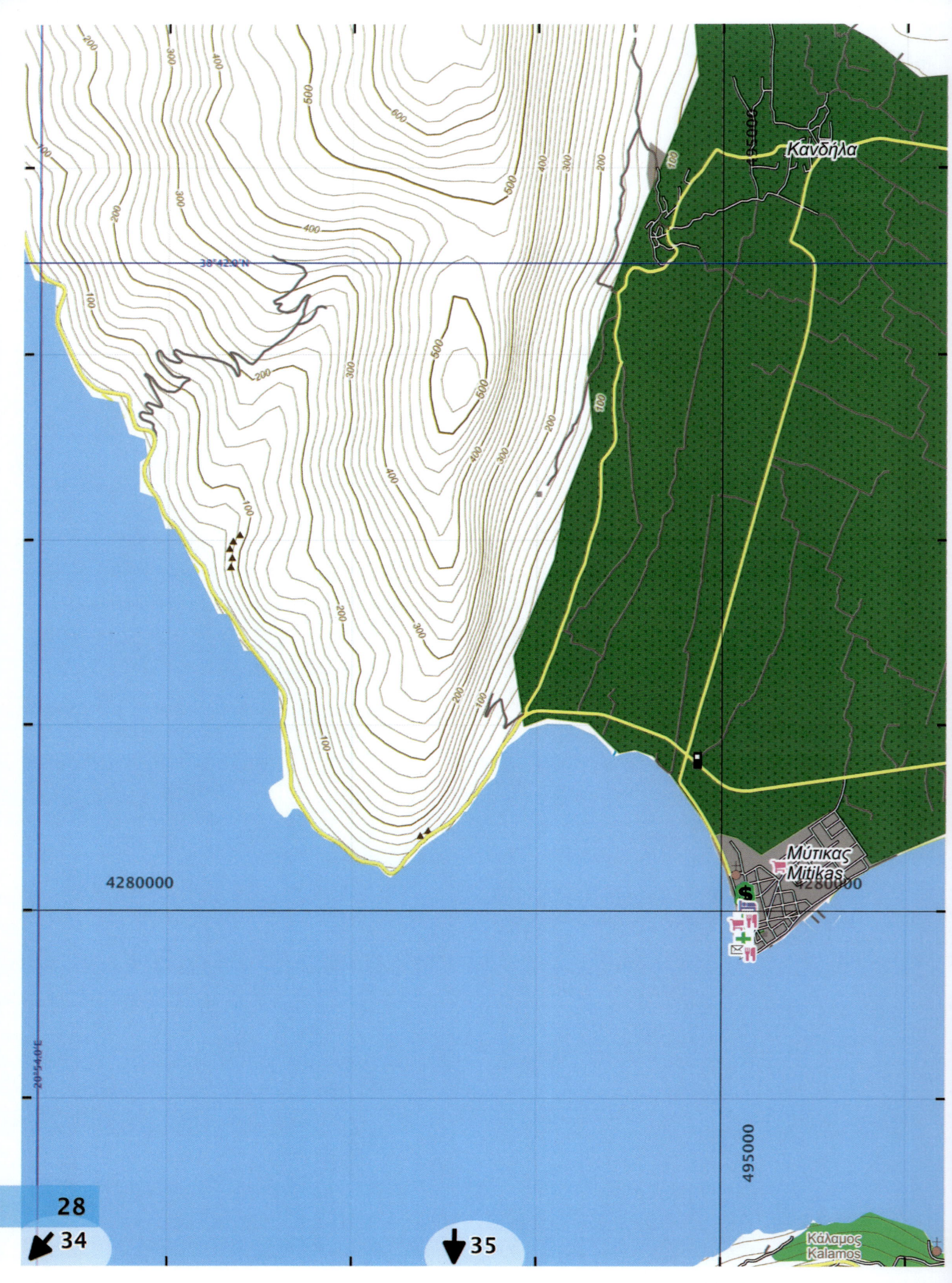

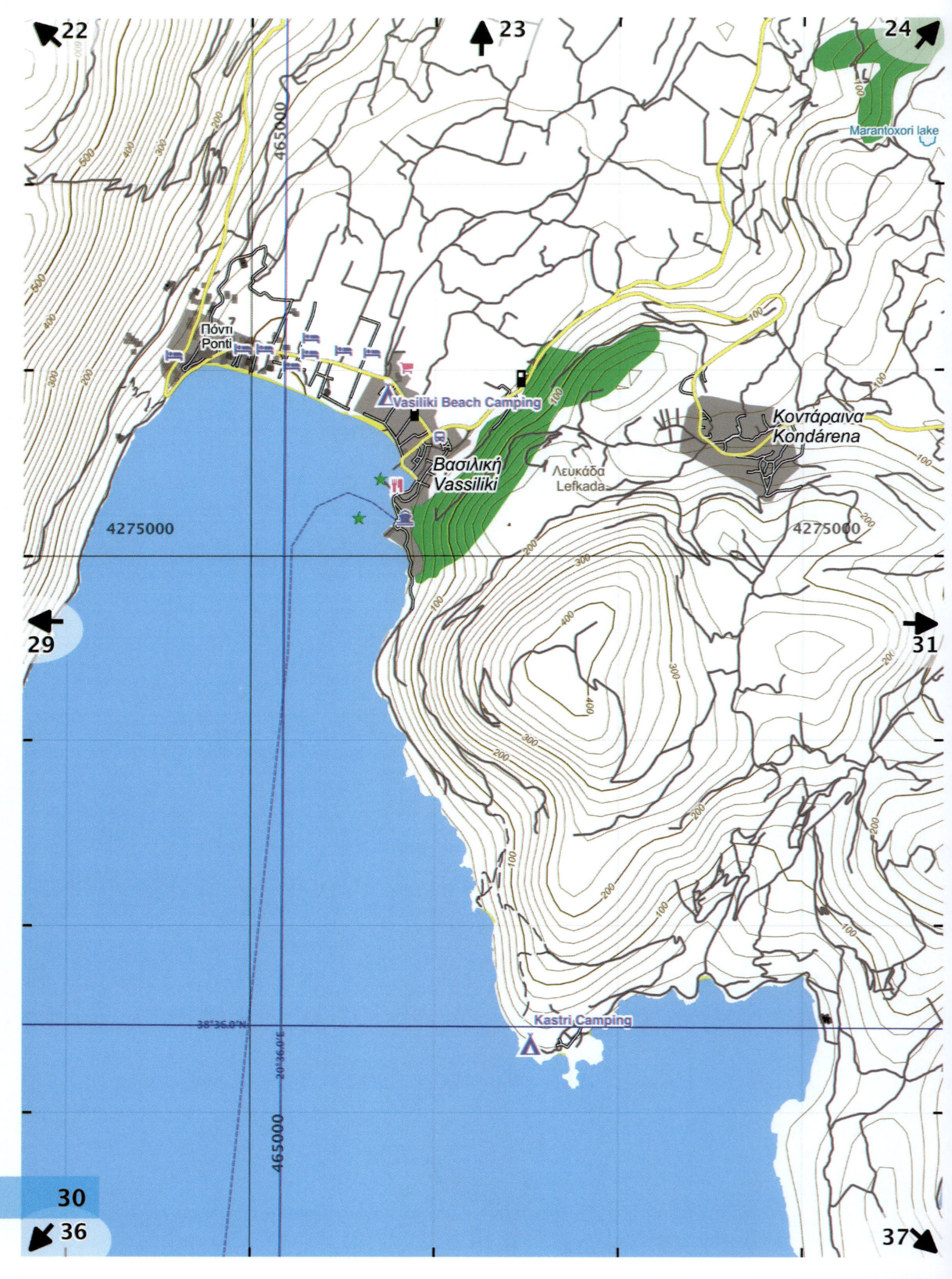

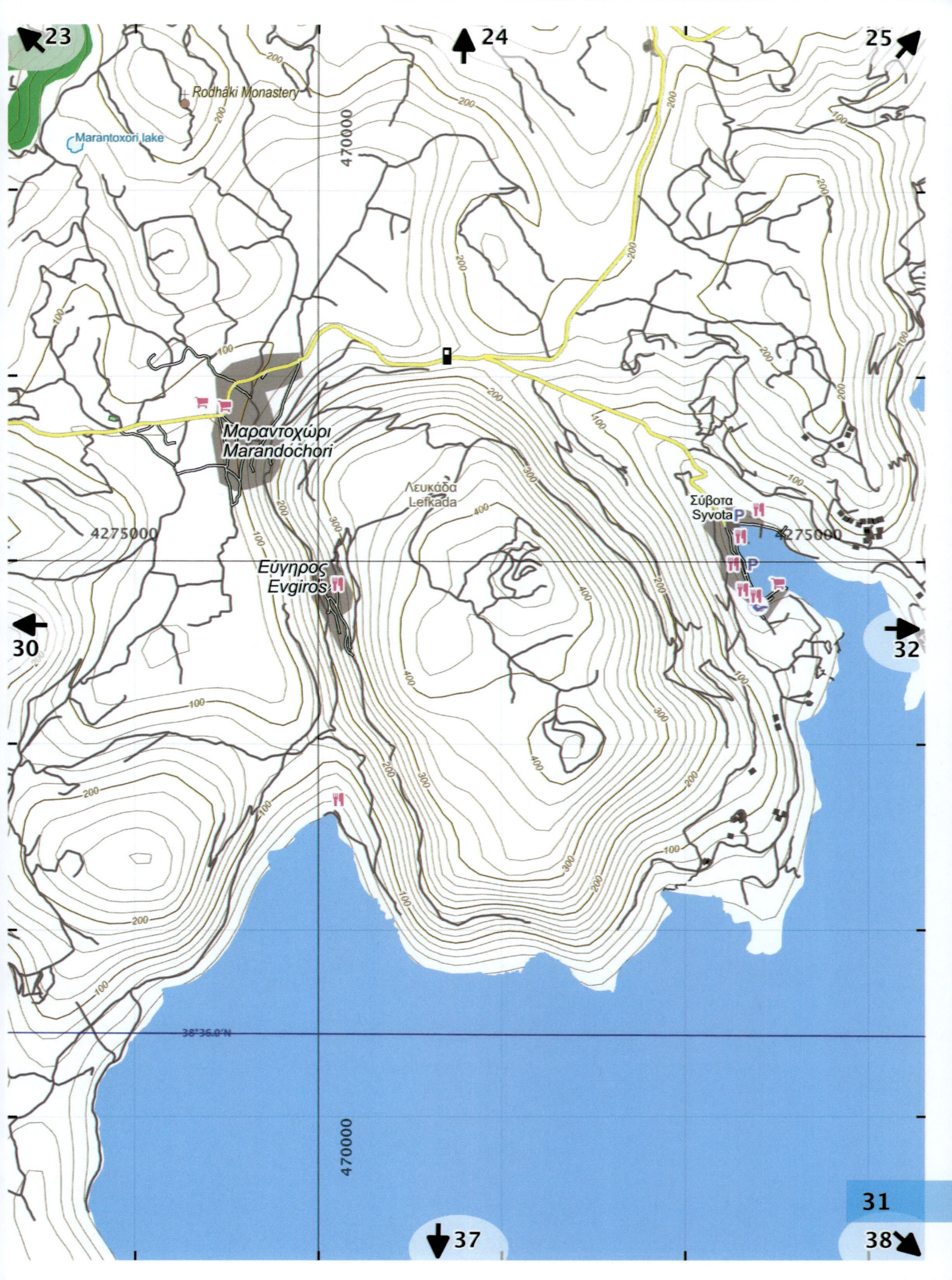

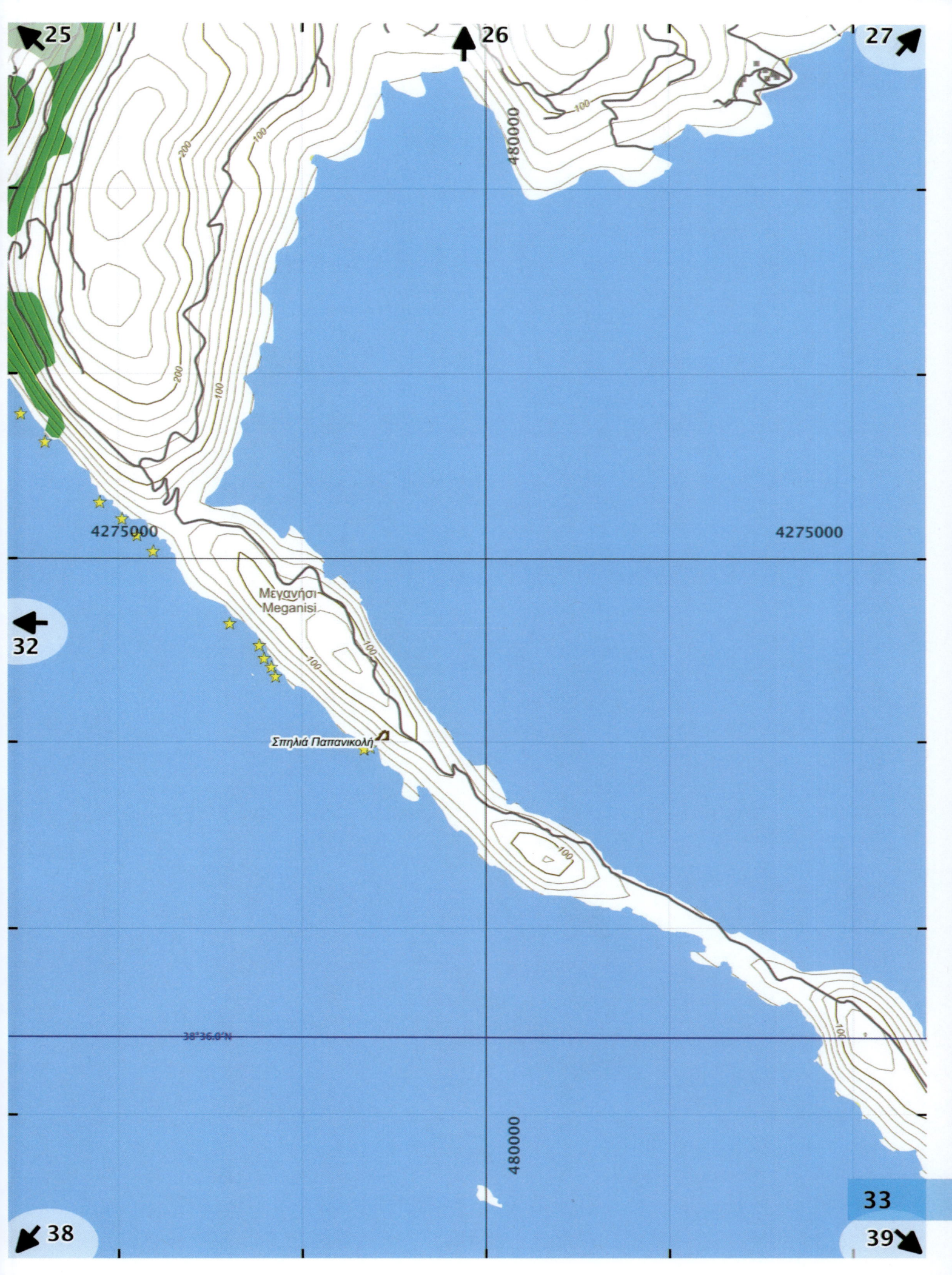

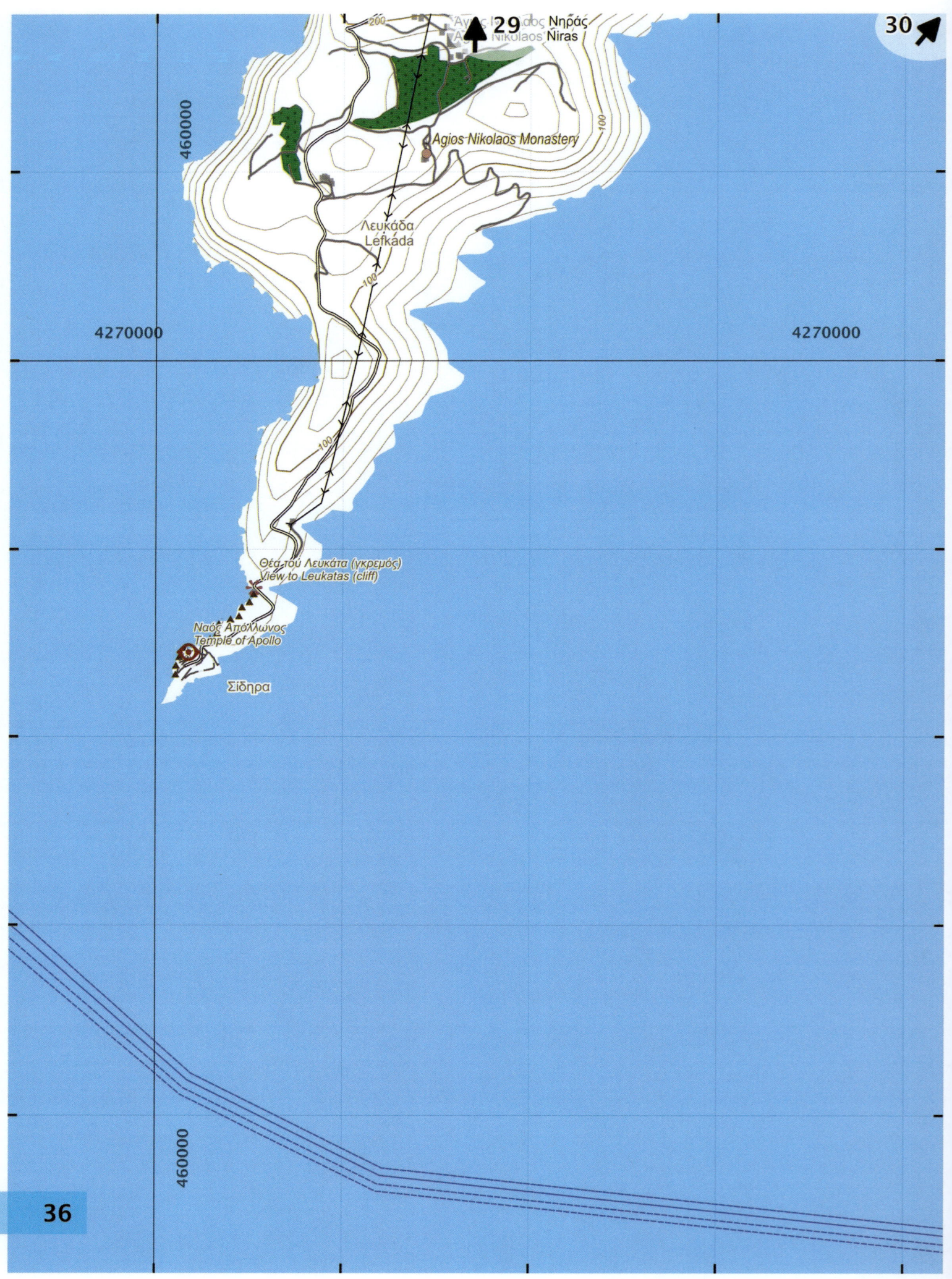

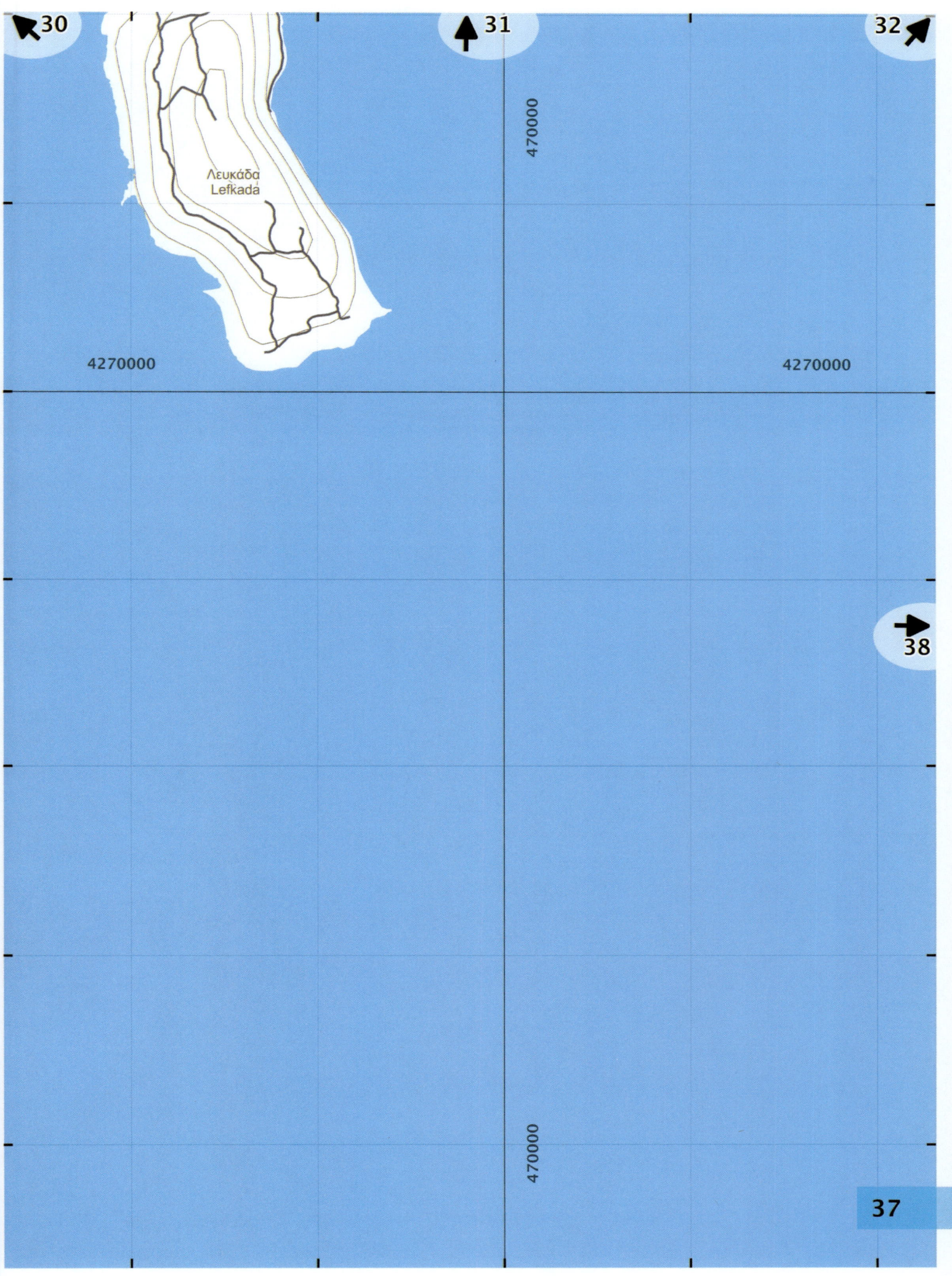

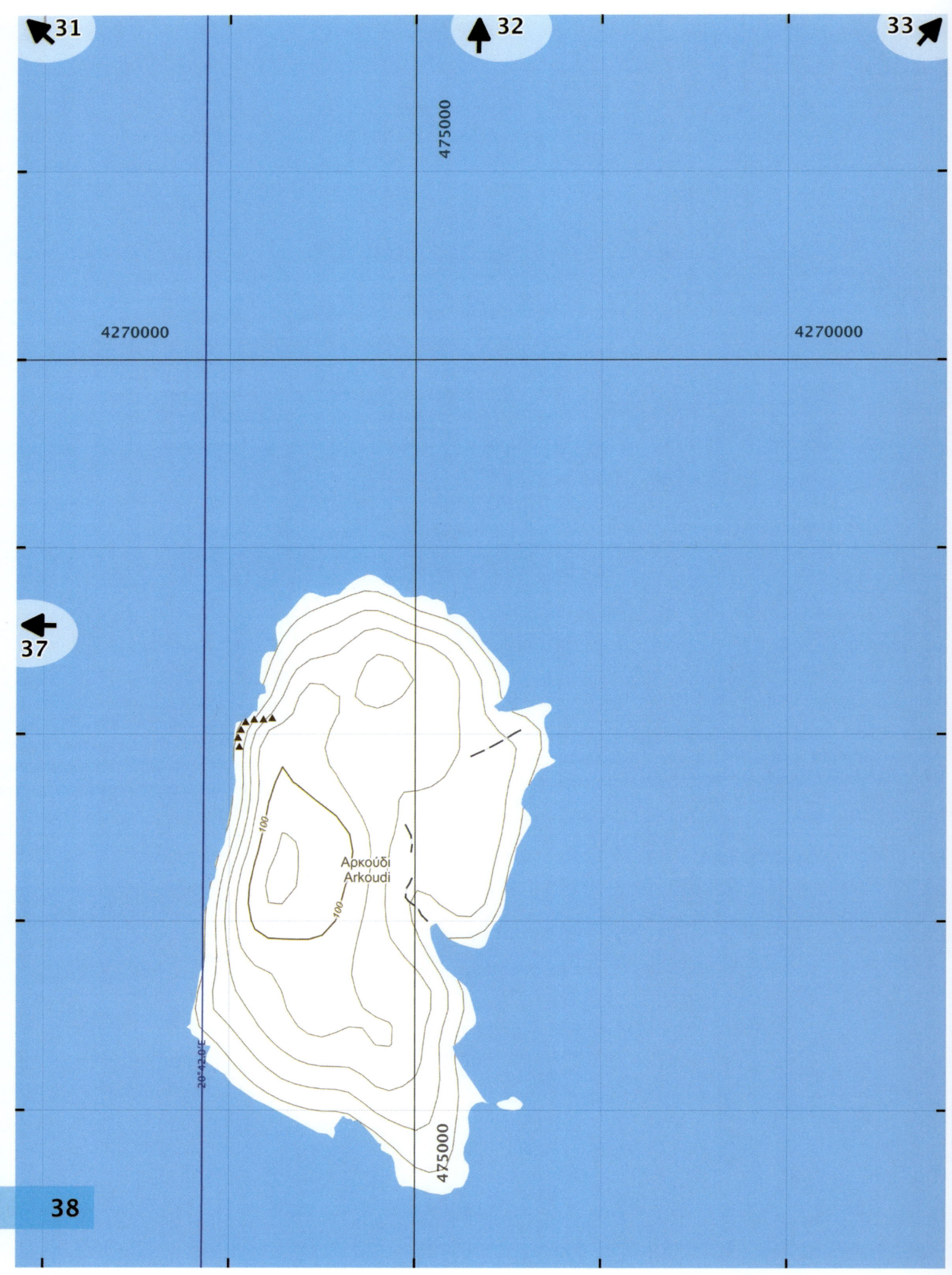

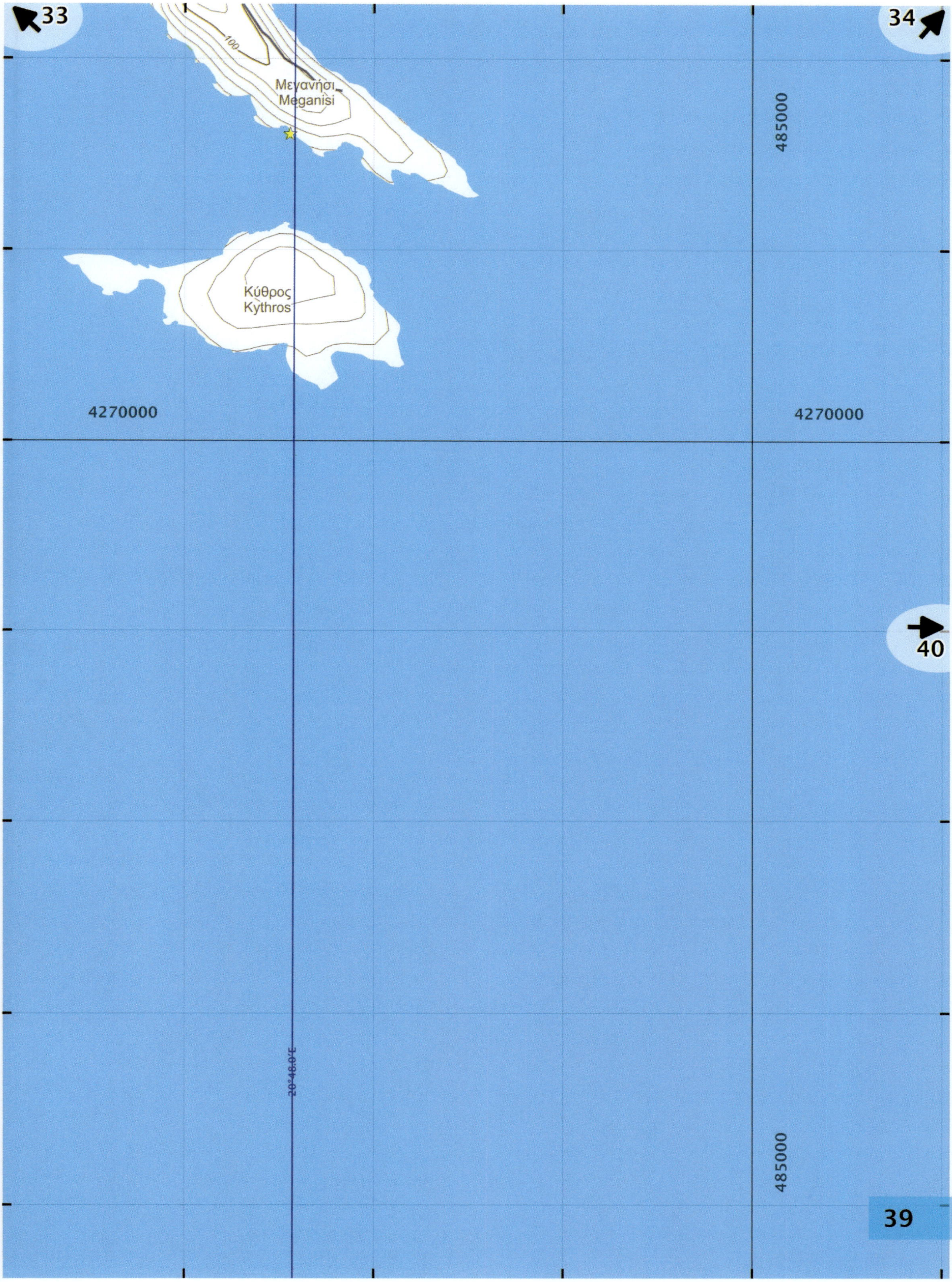

Μεγανήσι
Meganisi

Κύθρος
Kythros

4270000

4270000

485000

485000

20°48'0"E

33
34
40
39

No Warranty: This map is provided to you "as is," and you agree to use it at your own risk. The publisher and its licensors make no guarantees, representations or warranties of any kind, express or implied, arising by law or otherwise, including but not limited to, content, quality, accuracy, completeness, effectiveness, reliability, merchantability, fitness for a particular purpose, usefulness, use or results to be obtained from this map product, This map product is intended to be used only as entertainment and a supplementary travel aid and must not be used for any purpose requiring precise measurement of direction, distance, location or topography. The publisher makes no warranty as to the accuracy or completeness of the map data in this map product.

Map & Atlas Design Copyright © Sergio Mazitto Topo Maps, 2018

Some map data Copyright © Openstreetmap contributors

Published by Sergio Mazitto

Printed in Great Britain
by Amazon